Why Don't Elephants Live in the City?

By Katherine Smith

Consultant: Nicola Davies

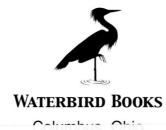

WATERBIRD BOOKS

Columbus, Ohio

Mc Graw Hill Children's Publishing

This edition published in the United States of America in 2004 by
Waterbird Books
an imprint of McGraw-Hill Children's Publishing,
a Division of The McGraw-Hill Companies
8787 Orion Place
Columbus, Ohio 43240-4027

www.MHkids.com

Library of Congress Cataloging-in-Publication Data is on file with the publisher.

First published in Great Britain in 2004 by *ticktock* Media Ltd.,
Unit 2, Orchard Business Centre, North Farm Road, Tunbridge Wells, Kent TN3 3XF.
Text and illustrations © 2004 *ticktock* Entertainment Ltd.
We would like to thank: Meme Ltd. and Elizabeth Wiggans.
Every effort has been made to trace the copyright holders, and we apologize in advance for any unintentional omissions.
We would be pleased to insert the appropriate acknowledgements in any subsequent edition of this publication.

Printed in China

1-57768-948-8

1 2 3 4 5 6 7 8 9 10 TTM 09 08 07 06 05 04

CONTENTS

Any words appearing in the text in bold, **like this**, are explained in the Glossary.

Why don't elephants live in the city?

Because elephants are the biggest land mammals on earth, and they need a lot of space!

Elephants live in family groups called **herds**. They roam the hot grasslands, forests, marshes, and deserts of Africa and Asia where there is plenty of room to move around!

There are usually about eight females, their young, and one male **bull elephant** in a herd.

Elephants share grasslands with zebras, giraffes, and rhinos.

African elephants have dips in their backs and are bigger than Asian elephants.

Human beings are the elephant's only **predator!**

Bull elephants often live in male-only herds or on their own.

Why don't elephants have small noses?

Because elephants need their long trunks to do many different things!

An elephant's **trunk** is actually its nose and top lip joined together. The elephant does not use its trunk just to smell and breathe! Think of all the ways you use your hand— to pick things up, to scratch your head, to touch, to hold, and to move things. Elephants use their trunks for all these tasks and many more!

An elephant can use its trunk like a hose. It can suck up and squirt water.

Elephants make loud trumpeting sounds with their long trunks.

Elephants can also use their trunks to breathe above water while they are swimming.

An adult African elephant's trunk is about 6 ½ feet long.

Why don't elephants have small ears?

Because elephants use their big ears to fan themselves in the heat.

Elephants also swim to cool off. They protect their skin from insects and sunburn by squirting water over their backs!

Elephants have long eyelashes to protect their eyes.

When facing danger, bull elephants stretch out their ears to make themselves look bigger and more threatening.

Every elephant's ears are unique. No two are alike.

Researchers believe elephants have good hearing and can "talk" to each other from far away.

Why don't elephants have smooth skin?

Because elephants need skin that bends and moves.

Imagine how hard it would be to bend your thumb without the stretchy wrinkles around the knuckle. Elephants are huge. Their skin needs to be really baggy and stretchy so that they can move easily.

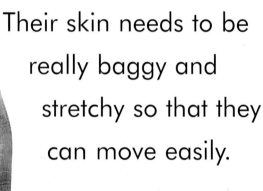
Elephants are born with wrinkled skin.

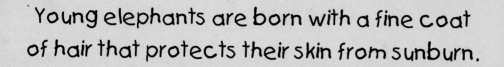

Young elephants are born with a fine coat of hair that protects their skin from sunburn.

Elephants have big, padded feet to support their enormous weight. This stops them from sinking into the ground.

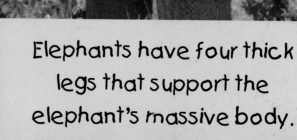

Elephants have four thick legs that support the elephant's massive body.

19

Why don't elephants have many calves at once?

Because calves stay with their mothers for many years and need a lot of care.

Elephants usually have only one calf every three or four years. Within a few hours of a calf's birth, it can stand and take milk from its mother.

Elephants have facial expressions that make it seem as if they are sad or happy.

Soon after a calf is born, the other elephants in the herd come to join it.

It takes time for the young calf to learn to use its trunk.

The only animal larger than an elephant is a whale.

Young elephants stay close to their mothers until they are about ten years old.

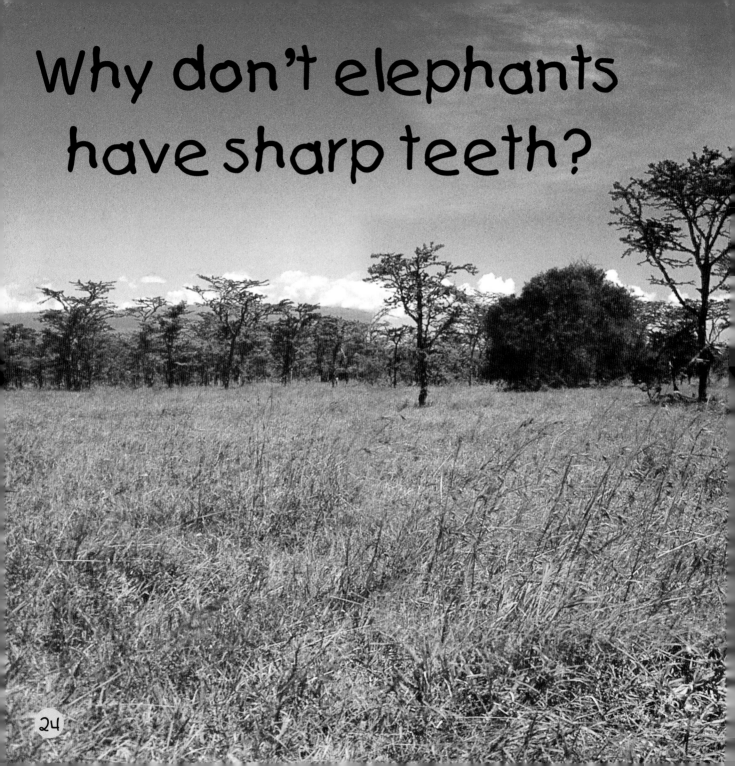

Why don't elephants have sharp teeth?

Because elephants are herbivores and don't need sharp teeth.

Elephants eat mainly leaves, grass, fruit, twigs, bark, and roots. They have four large teeth called **molars** for chewing and grinding up this tough food. Their **tusks** are long front teeth. Elephants use their front teeth for digging up roots and peeling off tree bark.

Elephants only attack other animals when they are threatened.

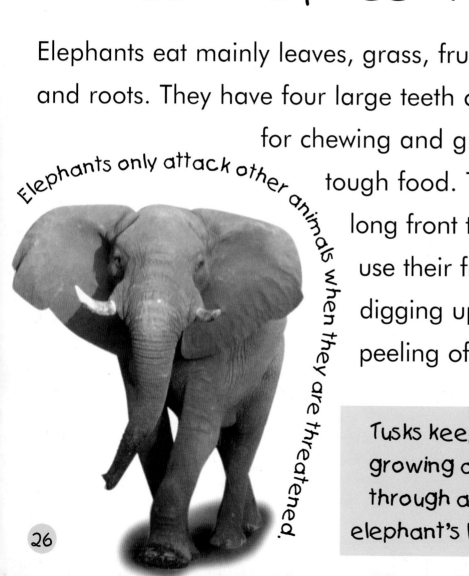

Tusks keep growing all through an elephant's life.

Elephants often break down trees in their search for food.

Each molar weighs as much as a brick!

27

Elephant PROFILE

Life span

70 years.

Size

10–13 feet tall. That is nearly twice as tall as a male human being!

Weight

An adult male weighs 13,000 pounds, which is more than the weight of four cars!

Numbers

There are estimated to be 300,000 to 600,000 African elephants and 35,000 to 50,000 Asian elephants.

Asia

Africa

Elephants live in Asia and Africa.

Fact file

Elephants can breathe through their trunks when they swim.

Elephants eat up to 1,000 pounds of food in a day and drink 30–50 gallons of water.

Elephants use the same paths year after year as they march across the wide, open spaces looking for food and water.

Elephants make waterholes in dry riverbeds. Other animals use these waterholes as well.

GLOSSARY

Bull elephant
The name for an adult male elephant.

Calves
The name for baby elephants. It is also used for the young of cattle, whales, and other animals.

Herds
Groups of animals that live and eat together.

Mammals
Animals that are warm-blooded and produce milk for their young.

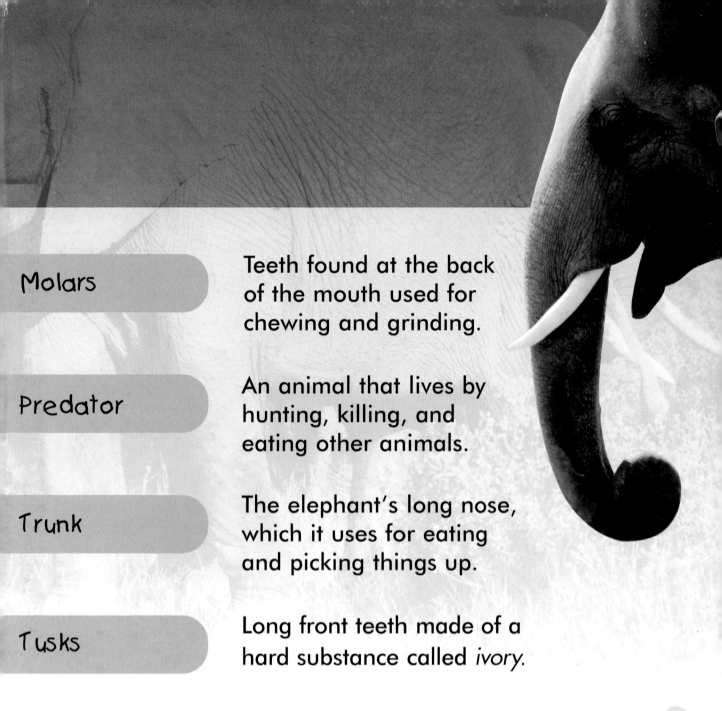

Molars

Teeth found at the back of the mouth used for chewing and grinding.

Predator

An animal that lives by hunting, killing, and eating other animals.

Trunk

The elephant's long nose, which it uses for eating and picking things up.

Tusks

Long front teeth made of a hard substance called *ivory*.

INDEX